On Reflection

By the same author:

Poetry

To Thalia

Watermark

Open Water (Audio CD)

Phantom Limb

Concrete Tuesday

Anatomy of Voice

Numb & Number

Selected Poems

Mishearing

Fiction

Glissando: A Melodrama

Anthology

Contemporary Australian Poetry (
(ed. with M. Langford, J. Beveridge and J. Johnson)

Criticism

Grotesque Anatomies: Menippean Satire Since the Renaissance

Feeding the Ghost 1:

Criticism on Contemporary Australian Poetry
(ed. with A. Kissane and C. Rickett)

On Reflection

or

A Twenty-Twenty Vision

A Novelty

David Musgrave

PUNCHER & WATTMANN

First published in 2005, reprinted 201919
Published by Puncher and Wattmann
PO Box 279
Waratah NSW 2298

http://www.puncherandwattmann.com
puncherandwattmann@bigpond.com

NATIONAL
LIBRARY
OF AUSTRALIA

A catalogue record for this book is available from the National Library of Australia

ISBN   9781922186744

Cover image: still from Andrei Tarkovsky's *Mirror*

Cover design by David Musgrave

Printed by Lightning Source International

To my mother and to the memory of my father

I.M. Bill Maidment

Ты была
Смелей и легче птичьего крыла,
По лестнице, как головокруженье,
Через ступень сбегала и вела
Сквозь влажную сирень в свои владенья
С той стороны зеркального стекла.
Арсений тарковский, первые свидания

You were
Bolder and lighter than the wing
Of a bird, down stairs like vertigo
You ran over steps and led through
Humid lilacs into your domain
From that side of the looking glass.

Arseny Tarkovsky, "First Meetings"

Transient flesh and the buds of death
bloom on mercator window-panes, rippled
in convex heat, off on the dark road
of the shivering heart of ugliness
for the soft glimpse of cragged basins
of the south where porpoises gnash
water, blind fists whacking the shimmered
plate of sea unblinking, melting
into mirrors like that abstract desolation,
for months that ogle each other,
wondering but knowing how it will stop
in that creased night of chance
when the mice will leap and dance.

He walks across the road and sees his distorted reflection in a shop-front window. As with all grotesqueries, the tenor of his thoughts turns toward the pastoral and the eternally returning wake of cyclical death and heat. At this juncture comes the realisation that thoughts leading from each other and about each other have a morbidity that can only be resolved by an awkward humour that never fails to value the importance of stupidity as a guiding principle at all the critical cusps of life. Consequently, when he returns home, instead of writing he plays a mindless computer game.

Borne up and strewn with petals of decay,
their fleshy odour mourning the slow passage
through the dying day,
scattered by the failing breeze,
tottering from side to side,
carried by weak, sunburnt hands
to that narrow bower where the thin trees hum
and camellias lie bruised in falling light,
soft onto that mound where the cool grass spreads
and the ants already with their furtive gifts
begin their slow campaign, enveloped in
that cloudless afternoon, their frail embrace
about those hollow sockets in that grim face.

The death of yet another chance to snatch motivation from the jaws of sloth proves to be the inspiration for a reverie concerning the cinematic ritual and sensuality of a hero's death. Of course, he is his own hero, fighting virtual demons in the hope that he may get his dignity back, or at least an ideal free lunch. As is to be expected, closure proves elusive and death less than final: yet again the computer has defeated him. Inexorably, his thoughts turn to love.

A somersault in time, beyond the need
again to find another soul, instead
the intimacy of fingernails, the solitude
of tea. The cardboard cut-out past
has filled and floated free above
warm bricks cooling in deluded
afternoons, unashamedly, transparently,
in jars and clothes and love-sick cupboards,
whining in unsung songs and swathed
on the carpet. How you would like
to dance in the clandestine room
with alabaster ceilings and unguent
mood music piped in subtle waves
and the ways of the world nowhere to be seen.

His first love, as he recalls less and less frequently, was a somewhat confused individual who agonised over a period of years between suffering a father for her child and freely following the callings of desire. Eventually she chose the latter, more out of tiredness and anger than actual fear. Life is such... but the different dimensions of remembered and anticipated love strike him as curiously antithetical: as he buys a sausage roll for lunch he is buoyed by the rich hope the future holds, while at the same time the love he lived gnaws at the back of his head like Ugolino.

Caught in the static thrill where waves repeating
roll through black afternoons, the clouds a cascade
of chance, spreading with needled lightning, lifting
the curtains on secret pleasures and pain
as if the wind did not remember blowing on that
hollow loss: a small girl lifting herself
up out of the bath, her fledgling hair
slicked back and ringlets of steam abundant.
But the brilliance of 'now' shines like
suns breaking through dismal clouds;
the chill remains, the awful recollections
of beauty somehow still forever bursting
fresh on splendid wet roads, glistening
trees and raindrops laughing down, just once.

Later in the afternoon a storm begins to break and the tempest outside matches his own inner turmoil (clichés, like insecurities, abound). As therapy he tries to write a poem, but cannot get beyond the image of a string of sausages. Instead, memories of unhappiness abound: his 'daughter' whom he has not seen for years and who probably no longer remembers him, but whom he loved more than he cares to express − the joke, of course, being that despite his heartbreak she is not even properly 'his', that biological boast. The usual restlessness strikes, and he has no choice but to wander outdoors for a while.

lace-fringe of tide
       flooding
the whelming of sea
       wrack
fleecing the sand, breasts
       become
waves, riding through
       tide
of womb, deep green
       diving
down where there is no
       light
where with pearl eyes
we shall live under water

Walking along, he thinks of an old chestnut: who would he have with him on a desert island, shipwrecked for eternity with mounds of mangoes and a bonanza of bananas? Even better than a servile cripple (you taught me language!) would be the light of his life, his imaginary ideal companion, the actuality of whom, of course, is as difficult to realise as it is to flesh out a poem, glimpsed rarely and mostly stinking of possessiveness or drowned in the slime of revenge. The scenery that greets him on his stroll is not much better. He turns for home no less agitated than when he set out.

Food not quite forgotten bubbles in the pot
and leaplet spurts of steamy water splash
the kitchen wall. Everything is stained
with hunger; curtains that nibble at the breeze,
windows that devour the view and vacuum
cleaners that would eat a house.
But there is always the mouthful after the last
or the aphrodisiacal beauty of feast after feast
of connivance with the world. Such generosity
does not stop at left-overs of the past
but fills with love the soon to be, and here
the kitchen is in perfectly random order and
the bubbling bump and hissing of pots
ring with the laughter of cannibals.

It is time that he ate something. He pulls out a few vegetables, some rice and a small sliver of meat on the turn and manages to prepare some kind of dinner. As he cooks, he takes part in the inevitable ritual of food as love, eating as communion, feast as celebration. His spirits rise, then sink as he simultaneously celebrates the intimacy of cooking with the solitude of serving for one. It is not a bad meal either, the unusual plenitude of fennel lifting the banal flavours into something like the sublime.

Standing in the middle of your field, counting
birds falling through air, the lustful croak
of frogs, spying the omen of wind mounting
hills, bustling through old gums and an oak.
In the middle of your field eggs are hatching
and sprung blossoms shower to the ground:
there is time for eating ripeness, watching
the arrow of your smile, your mound.
From there ride high over whole vistas of birth
to the ocean edge, the simple slap,
rush, licking your toes, the grainy, naked earth
swelling under the deep, dimpled flaps
of fleshy waves folding in to shore,
rolling into a distant, warming roar.

As he eats his thoughts turn to the subject of fornication – Phwoar! But of course, the act of love is multidimensional – on occasions it can, he believes, smash through the ego barrier, but mostly it's drunken distrust and desire, the old to and fro, my god is that the time, you remind me of someone else, oops, sorry I will call, you do have protection don't you? Just slip on your sunglasses and pretend nothing's happened, even though somewhere inside is a vacant, mangled silence. The mood seizes him to have a night out on the town.

The dead are living in reverse, spiralling
back through malbowges, through the avenues
of hell back to that throttled gasp where hope
escaped and the fears and desires of those
still living clotted in an instant
dissolved in a chasm of time, within
which fortune waits on disaster, huddled
like a cunning rat, falling like
an afternoon where death has failed to leave
its mark, instead impressing scents on cars,
the failed telephone call, the elusive taxis
with bone-grim drivers searing past lonely
gutters at 3am; all a part
of that fantastic dance, that backward glance.

He is tired, it is late, to be going home is the least desirable option, but opportunity mocks. Actually, home is preferable to strange spunks' beds or the couch of insensibility. He decides to flip a coin: heads he will go home, tails he will go to the late closing pub. The coin falls down the drain and he interprets this as a promising sign. He walks home, determined to save money and ignore the houri-like taxis that flit by, beckoning. The walk is long, paradoxically compounding both thirst and fatigue. By way of compromise, he buys a bottle of ginger beer from the 7-11 on the homeward stretch.

Revert, abstract and feel fantastic for whole
days free from the taint of failure and free
from tongues chanting mantras,
seeing things in rocks, refusing white slippers.
If you do not, the grotto will close, denying
all images, shutting out those breezy
observances that come from air and the rhythm
of trees. The beyond is impossible to reach:
slinking shadows disappear with the day,
falling on lucid ponds and over leaves
infested with snails slowly mutilating
subtle shades, echoes of that voice
that comes from nowhere, rending all
that once seemed strange and magical.

Not being all that tired, he stays up late to watch a film about Saint Bernadette of Lourdes. She believes in the visions she has had in a grotto, just as he once emphatically believed in a world of the mind and used to be able to assert this belief with conviction. She refuses to wear white slippers to the grotto, as he refuses to call himself 'poet.' Perhaps the grotto is like that cave which is full of images but really a negative of how we are. It is beautiful, but such beauty is not like other forms of beauty that we deem 'good'. Rather, it is a revelation of banality, mortality and tiredness. Time for bed.

Podsnap to barstool, skunked in gimcrack hotels
with the remembrance of that wave of sickness,
Mexican style, inside the centrifuge where
fanciful outlines merge in violet richness.
Tip-toe to treetop, autumn flecks of lava
blazing in plumes of cocktail-coloured madness;
sepals unyielding, dense in foldless night of
camera-ready spurts of beauty flush with
fever-room outbursts stretched from thought to nightmare;
units of noise emerge like secret handshakes,
common enough but nothing more than islands,
pockets of forethought, outcrops, magma turned to
stone in the mouth of meaning, speechless tongues of
igneous petals grandly saying nothing.

He awakes not quite knowing where he is, although it is much like the half-dream room where the snakes squeal and the alligators blow trumpets. Of course, he is in his own bed and of course he is alone and slightly hungover, and he purposely slides into the semi-directed dreams, a grotesque of nightclubs and forests, volcanic lust and, if it is the case that some people can speak in tongues, hearing in ears. Eventually, sleep yields no more slack, and he must get up. He potters around, avoiding making his bed out of procrustination: that is, putting off making one's bed in case one has to lie in it. The fuzziness of his morning merges into a general fuzziness, around which he cannot seem to find his way.

Life is the reluctant carnival,
upside-downness for the sake of escape.
What else but an uproar of images
kicking out words and desires
could become the goose-bump parade,
cross-purposed and chatterboxing,
jumping up and down with delight?
Soon it will all end for the days
which are unavoidable, the story
of bread and butter, the flames of winter evenings.
From the moment we love such images
they cease to be mere facts
but bits of beauty cheap as chips
and really, really, true.

It could, however, be worse – an amputation or permanent, rather than temporary, brain damage. Other people, or at least some of them, are always worse off (because they are not him?). But maybe there are some who fear nothing, dangerous doppelgängers always just ducking out of sight. Maybe one such as this has snaffled up the 'ideal future' he has hoped and planned for himself. Isn't that from a 50s science fiction movie? He breakfasts in the unforgiving light of mid-morning and plans his day.

Death is my friend, he will come to me whispering
tinkerbell sunset flamingo thrills,
happily thrashing his feelings about
like an inexplicably beached whale.
He will come on a tip-toe jinking run
with mad-cap words explainable to children,
the question of a dark funeral in my
teacup on Tuesday on his horrible lips.
He will play charades and mime those emotions
that can't really be understood, those unread
books and unreadable, unnecessary
confessions, the death's head grin of dawn.
He will come like the tide, ruthlessly
sneaking up the old suburban canal.

He has to drive to the library to return some overdue books; otherwise he won't be allowed to borrow the books that he really wants to read. As he searches for a parking spot and is increasingly irritated at the difficulty of finding one, he is relieved to stumble upon the comparison of death with parking: viz., death is something (if you're lucky) that won't take a great deal of effort on your part, unlike parking. This makes him feel better about his frustration. When he gets to the library it is closed, it being a public holiday. He slips the books down the after hours chute and then goes shopping.

Experience is cheap and wisdom
cheaper by the dozen, slung
on racks or in bins or hung on whitewashed
walls, whole percentages stripped
revealing patent lies and secret
values known only to winkers
and the markets of the heart.
Coins are digital, notes analog,
and tumbling out of catalogues
possibilities astound, what they teach
and what they leave unspoken.
Fingers flash over counters
while outside the door the rumbling
juggernauts terrorise the road.

At the local shops, being careful to avoid the awful honesty of mirrors, he is delighted and enraptured by the poetry of commerce. Fuck art when you can make a million bucks and have a permanent tan and have your own skin cancer specialist on call. Although he doesn't quite have that much money, he visits the delicatessen where he used to take his 'daughter' shopping. The experience is not entirely unpleasant, retail therapy he supposes, as he buys chocolate as a gift for his girlfriend when he sees her later that night.

Denying thoughts as if they could become
the stalking present, the cat that waits to slash
air and tear on flesh thoughtfully:
we have our little times and kindnesses,
those slightly sozzled evenings where we share
half-concealed, half-conspiring things
like childhood pets, swelling curves and sounds
that we might have liked to hear, but don't.
In fact, the rapid shadows of our words
loiter in the margins where familiar
thoughts will not follow, tailing
desire and slyly catching at
curtains and those hints that pass between us
like the transit of a shy Venus.

Actually, that's not really true — his 'girlfriend' has placed the relationship firmly on a 'special friends' footing. She has a cat called Barry Pumpkin Bum who has in the past jumped on him while he's asleep. The next morning, while dreaming of houses and attractions, he wakes, startled by a sudden skittish pounce. Images from the dream quickly dissolve but they leave behind their powerful aura of unrestrained passion. For a while he is disoriented, unfamiliar with his mind until he fully wakes up. Then he accustoms himself to the ludicrous and impossible optimism of dream, forgets, showers and goes to work.

There are the secret nosepickers and those
who look as though they want it or wouldn't mind it
or are checking you out or being checked out
or are picking brains instead of noses.
Half a hundred bottoms bounce in time,
leaning into corners and holding in
their farts until the daily mass disgorgement.
However many hours spent behind
the girl with the axolotl eyes
could not be likened to antiseptic
minutes spent in waiting rooms or snacklets
of rare delight or hard to get at picnic
spots but is just like sitting behind
the girl with the axolotl eyes.

He catches the 8:15 bus, sitting in the same seat behind the same girl. He realises with a start that he has been doing this for too long, and that time spent on public transport is unlike any other time known to humanity. Everybody is, without doubt, obsessed with sex: what would happen if this bus suddenly ended up on a desert island? Who would be the winners and who the losers? However, these thoughts evaporate as soon as his stop comes up and it is back to 'real time' when he gets off the bus, forgets about the sort on the third window seat from the back on the left, and walks through the front door of work.

Hammerheaded,
enriching life away with videos
and books:
late for work again and again
against the grain
unpolished manners bristling with
mirrored rage
and out to lunch in surreal cafés
where dreadlocked waiters
prink and prance; and back to work in
the office chill
with smouldering stares and unconcern
that the door
is somehow more than just a door.

Unfortunately he is late yet again, tired and lacking in concentration. It would seem that he has been spending too much time enjoying himself. But, as his Irish friend keeps pointing out, "It's all very funny until someone loses an eye." In this instance he is temporarily denied his livelihood as he is 'shown the door'. All is not lost – the severance pay is actually something to write home about. For a job he hated, he has certainly reaped some rewards. On the way home, he dines out in an expensive restaurant, buys himself some CDs, some new clothes and a book by an obscure French modernist.

Time wasted is time gained for the almost
endless splurge through dim-lit nights where time
is a schooner filling and draining, swum in the smoke
that is the burning of lost souls calling
across that dark divide: I am here, you will
join me, I am yet to come into being,
believe me, brain me, write me down on the back
of a coaster, sing me songs in the stumbling glide
back home where you tug on the light, scatter your clothes,
drink in the flicker of ghosts and flare of the tele,
an oracle within those scanning frames
that strain their light on oblongs of paper, white
with the vacant shambles of this fumbled, festive night.

Unemployed at last! He feels reckless enough to go out drinking infeasible amounts of beer, ballooning his gut like a pregnant football. The narrative seems so clear: forget, or at least attempt to erase, but nevertheless he must acknowledge those bits inside him which he owns but cannot sell. Who would buy a tawdry cat fart? What price? Joan Crawford was such a glamour-puss. She might be dead, but at least she made money. He resolves to enter merchant banking, or management consultancy as a desperate second.

The calculus of steel and clichéd glass
seem not to matter: money is being made
and some people are happy. He is chuffed
at the fact that his shoes are admired for their shine
by an advertising buddha with one hand open,
one hand closed, telling him how to write
one open poem followed by one closed.
Young execs with anaconda ties
ponce around, peccadillionaires
with youth a figment to wangle for money
more than their noses can accommodate:
a fabulous future now staked for a stale
and cocky hope, to play the game and prosper
and age with graceful smarm, and bask in love.

Consequently, he attempts to plunge into the Jungle of Business, which at first glance would appear to be foolhardy. Appearances, of course, are always to be trusted, as that's all there is. One prospective employer is a prominent advertising executive who has subsequently made millions from writing fiction, appearing on talk shows and talking about the death of his son from AIDS. Despite the enormous heart of this man and the numerous promises he makes, the result is zip. Nevertheless, there is a dubious shine that remains to this whole strange episode.

The eminent poet sits humourless
in a pub of his own creating,
watching 'Instant Date' on SKY TV
as he contemplates his next batch of words
in fundamental forms that make his art.
The solar afternoon announces night
with one last blaze, illuminating white
pages over which his black pen glides.
Outside the pub is traffic. Exhausts fart,
the not-so-divine afflatus, sooty fumes
that creep up his trouser leg and settle
on his pompous bouffant. Some specks
scatter on the page, a potty logic
from which he tries hard to push out art.

He needs more money, however, and, since he thinks he can write poetry, he decides to apply for a fellowship, for which he requires references from three people. He sends a letter to an eminent poet who has written poems about French thinkers in Sydney pubs. Unfortunately, the honesty and consequent tactlessness of his humorous epistle (incautiously he refers to such begging letters as "brown-nosing") backfires. The poet replies contemptuously with phrases like "I pray to God you never get a book published" and "the poetry world is sick enough without people like you polluting it further." He takes this reply as a definite no.

Momentary madnesses distract us
from our deaths, in time and out of it
our loves that eventually will snarl
or bicycle the streets, ballooning with
abandon. What would we know: multiplied
absurdities careen our floating minds
and fill the past with horror. Descending as
we do, looking to our backs, adrift
where fell gusts blow racketeering,
our quarrels bunch before the infinite.
What we would, done in bloated vanity,
evaporates like mist; pain becomes
a cruising breaker, arching up, groping
down to the smash of its oblivion.

To make matters worse, he gets a telephone call out of the blue from his Irish friend, who tells him that he is persona non grata with a certain publisher. What could be the reasons, he distractedly asks himself; he hasn't the faintest idea. ("Like hell he does," glowers the publisher every time he sees him.) Perhaps such instances merely remind us of our own absurd stupidities, when in actual fact we should be down at the beach with a few stubbies and a volume of Voltaire, some prawns and a beach ball. He looks forward to the sensual indulgences of summer.

He calls his brother to check up on the family and is caught by surprise. His father is in hospital, it is not known how serious his condition is. He drives like a demon for almost an hour before he reaches the hospital, where he is told his father died earlier that afternoon. His grief remains unrecorded, one of those moments that cannot be heightened or diminished by the embellishment of words. Needless to say, it is painful and surreal, both of which qualities become less apparent with the passing of time. It is as if the rest of his life has begun under the most dreadful of auspices.

Where does pain come from?
Where does the moon go
with measured delight,
in dayspring drunken spirals
or nightly masculine silence?
How does it manage to follow you
when you are driving in your car?
Why do days follow each other? How is it done?
Why is the sun like a woman?
Why is light so honest, or totally absent,
doled out with care, like pleasurable food,
the banquet of our arrogance, or fear?
Another time and place suggests itself
where the cost of living still remains too high.

He returns indefinitely to the family home until the rituals of death have been laid out and put to rest. In the end he is perturbed by those out-of-syntax questions that occasionally benumb the consciousness: and then what? Or, what difference does it make? He retreats from the everyday and prefers to wallow in cosmic conjecture: the sky, the stars, wind, water and rocks have about them as much pathos as can be tolerated. And then he wakes in the middle of the night unaccountably sobbing until he remembers the death that weighs so heavily, day in, day out.

Prone to tears and boredom because summer
was not extraordinary, peeled back
like an afternoon hat, survivor of heat
and unseasonal winds, like friendliness,
fresh and unforgotten. Out of sorts
later that night, darkness piles on cool
tea leaves pungent in secret diagonal
gardens sprayed with kamikaze beetles.
From the hidden corners odours grow:
bubblegum port-wine magnolia, privet
like rancid fat, the layered tannin, hopeless
dandelion aglow with twilight breeze.
Even on those days of total eclipse
dark fruit bursts like passion between your lips.

Despite grief, its process taking the course of any disease, that tarot joy of living still remains, even if the pleasure it offers is no longer familiar. There are some moments when he is hopelessly happy, balanced also by those moments on the edge of the pit. He is spending most of his time in unhappy holiday mode, mooning around his mother's house. He disappears from time to time into books, and sniffs the odours of the house that have long since ceased to be real, like the tumuli of tea leaves that cover the camellia bed.

For every action there is an equal and opposite
revulsion,
embryos in ultrasound,
serrated leaves that populate the picnic;
and for every slice of life
consumed –
medallions on a china plate,
time-lapsed growth and putrefaction
bound together in the ribboning mind –
another cut
in the adjectival theatre
going down the wrong way
and at another time altogether
made a meal of.

One night he watches a video of a contemporary movie that has putrefaction as one of its major themes. Even though the dialogue is terrible, he likes watching the maggoty images that pop up every few minutes. These, in turn are interspersed with documentaries about Life On Earth, and amputations. It makes fascinating viewing as he eats his dinner. After a few weeks of the cycle of videos, remembrance, comfort and pain, he decides it is time to return to his own home and resume the practice of everyday life.

Maps of Ireland are quilted on the bed
under moth infested light-shades casting
uncertainty on ochre patches. It takes
an Irishman, an immigrant escapee
and catch-purse victim of parental
pain, to point this out and laugh. Sloppy
lives lead to spilt ends. Demanding
answers only asks more questions, ping-pong
introspections: Oh dear. These lines
refuse to snug themselves; whatever problems
stream unconsciously will not be dammed
by words alone. There are those bad habits
that parody life, and those parodies
that take us back to where it all began.

His Irish friend pays him a visit and is anxious for a beer. His friend sits on the bed, impatiently waiting for him to ready himself for an unaccustomed social outing. Unfortunately, the quilt cover is in the wash, and evidence of involuntary bodily detrusions embarrasses them both to laughter. With this he realises one of the bases for their friendship: shared horror stories of attempted parenting, his lost 'daughter' and his friend's daughter, the custody of whom is currently being decided by the courts. But these things are not to be spoken of, particularly when they are about to go out and detonate a few brain grenades.

Dissent is like a poisoned alphabet
that spells the names of multiplied obsessions
speckling the refrigerator door.
Their messages reflect the accidents
of time and space: the algebra of distance
and the arguments of broken memory
quarrel on the page like yowling cats.
This disagreement turns on decadence,
as with poetry, dedicated
to those lazy cracks that act out
passions, tranquilized politenesses
and callous insincerities calmly
placed upon the page, miraculously
taking on the semblance of a life.

The next day he gets a postcard from his brother who has just arrived in Korea for an intensive language course. "Ah Seoul!" he reads and sticks it on the fridge next to the other cards from Paris, Tokyo, New York and Newcastle NSW. He enjoys reading them almost as much as he enjoys writing and sending them, his preferred medium being the back of a beer coaster. Along with the postcard comes a telephone bill and a letter offering him a job at a nearby university. It's only casual tutoring, but he can't complain. In fact, thanks to the incompetency of the university administration, the letter gives him only a week's notice. He decides to see the place the following day, ironing a shirt and having an early night so that the visit to his new place of employment cannot possibly go wrong.

"Come out to play," the little voice will say
that is not so little really but is shrill
and busting to crush snails and prove the lies
of generality "always on the run"
cruelled beyond belief over the fence
and under the trees into the brown river
wading and feeling for reeds and things that bite
and the promise that finite blue extends: it might
be fine or the day may be the giver
of a bounty of water falling in dense
bundles shattering on grilled roads the sun
has loved and left and before too long will rise
up and over the four-foot distant hills
and smile superior smiles on another day.

The scenery at this new university is stunning, with the mountains to the west and rolling paddocks nestling the small, budding buildings of the campus. He is uplifted by the 'clean' air, the prospect of having money again and the general hopefulness that floods through him each time he begins a new job. In fact, the absence of pessimism (he usually describes this to himself as 'negative optimism') recalls, of all things, the exploratory expeditions of childhood. By the time he returns home he feels ready to face anything.

Out on a windy day
with moistening air and the hum of heat –
clouds like brains
get ready, set and
blow their wet violence
on the small stone garden
where fine white ash lifts
and moves about in fancy shapes
collapsing into runnels of fallen rain.
The car that takes us home
is like a spaceship
oiled on wheels of air
and, as we drive, ahead of us
another lucky dog crosses the road.

The time has finally come for his family to scatter his father's ashes. He drives with his brother and mother out to the crematorium, where they try to collect the ashes. Unfortunately, it is the weekend and there is only one person in attendance and she is on her tea break. When the attendant finally returns they collect the ashes, take them to a small round garden where the ominous clouds finally decide to unchain the rain that has threatened all day. Totally drenched (tears as well as rain) and having scattered the ashes they drive home in an unreal, bitter calm, just missing a dog crossing the road.

Driving by the inductive method past
a dingy rind of beach that dries, then wets —
undulating hills of grass empathic
with the heat sway delicate sways
in a drive-by tourist way... the heat
swims in exotic strokes past the horizon,
above the panicky back-burning, afraid
of dryness and air-conditioning, conceit
out of control around a hairpin bend
and then the condescending street signs, clouds
unlike the clouds left behind obvious
to the gaze. Ordinary things
become the stranger, psychic card machines
and politics, the game playing of dreams.

Shortly afterwards he gets a phone call from the country. He is invited to stay with friends in a country town and he drives up the next day choosing the old road. Summer is in its infancy and is understandably uncontrollable, indulging in a tantrum of heat. Eventually he begins the descent into the happy valley, arriving at the pub at 3pm. He meets a man who shares his passion for beer and gambling. They discuss recent commonwealth legislation until his friends pick him up and take him home.

Everything must have a name: the ant's pants,
the termite's trousers, that acme of acne, the moon.
There are right-handed feelings and left-handed feelings
and ambidextrous thoughts of great cunning.
There are objects in the dative case
and actions that assume a feminine form.
There are names of names of names of names
and fish and empty windows and those full.
There are days obsessed with the memory of smell
and curves of various velocity.
There is the irritating need for food
and a modicum of space and peace and quiet.
Obviously, life is so wonderful
it's a wonder everyone has not been driven mad.

He resolves never again to use the first person pronoun in any future poems, a determination arrived at after socialising with his friends, drinking, playing games, talking about incunabula and becoming rather appalled at the inescapable necessity to assert one's self, even if it only takes the form of defending one's head against an angry pool cue in the local pub. Generally, he observes that he has not laughed so much in months and is overwhelmed by the feeling (deluded) that he has escaped. He drives back home via the same circuitous route and drops in on his mother on the way.

Leaves stick and burrs scratch.
Water runs in slimy films down sandstone
rocks where spiders bloat in crazed webs
waiting to drop down the back of a fifteen year old,
stalking flesh and those soft parts which have
no meaning, blank and caring little
about death, plunging their fangs into
slim curves yet to crust and age,
wreaking the logic of 'here we are,
and that's the way it goes, big nose,' losing
that last preserve against decay, carried away
to the smooth smelling afternoons where food
is on heat and what is to come hangs pendulous.

His mother is, as usual, graciously critical and he is pleased by the pleasure his visit seems to bring. After the usual question and answer session, he goes for a walk, passing his childhood haunts. He sees the bush and remembers the time he slid down a rock, punctured his thigh on a stick and became entangled in a spider's web. These thoughts are, in turn, entangled with a nostalgia for a time of anticipation, which has now become a mute acceptance. He turns back and has dinner with the agèd P and ends up staying the night to save a bit of money.

ash like butterflies
        oven air
the personality of heat –
the trees are sullen and funereal
            the sky is gaping
        reddish haze and
mazed shadows harrow the ground
insects seem afraid –
            cicada nymph dirt bubbles
crunch underfoot as the backyard bakes.
When the smoke comes
the house is sunk in rusty light
and like the Martians we've become
it's up and away on a hellfire day.

In the morning, ash from a back-burning operation settles on the backyard and the patio. Unlike the remains of his father this ash has a life, warm and floating through the air. Later in the day they learn that what began as precautionary back-burning has escalated into a full-scale fire raging across the bushland of the city. The neighbours are already cleaning their gutters in a panicked way and hosing down their roofs (not thinking of the water pressure). His mother has packed a few bags, including the photo albums, and left them next to the car, just in case.

If it isn't one thing it's another,
laughter without end, enough to make a cat speak.
And, if the door does not stay shut, it opens
on an inside that has shrunk and an
outside that cannot be admitted:
gnocchi clouds float in a blue soup,
white noise in the television sky;
a high wind flays the trees
and papers inside scatter and reel.
It is like a double dream, that which is written
and that which we dream of as we write.
In the end, in the dark, it may be the case
that a lonely figure is out there, somewhere,
throwing stones from the outskirts of night.

The bushfires have spared them this time and once the ashes have been raked from the garden life appears almost normal. Everything reminds him of everything else, so he makes an effort to try and pin a bit of certainty onto the world. Neither astrology nor alienation, speculation nor chiromancy can provide the spur he needs to seize his life by the scruff of the neck and toss it out on the street where it probably belongs. He returns to his squalid little flat for the start of a new week.

The wind will have its way with the trees
and underwear as usual will wave
hysterically from the washing line.
Twenty reasons for emigrating descend
like social climbers upon the letterbox,
unsigned valentines and library fines.
A cat betrays defiance and a secret
source of electricity in leaps,
whirrs, static fur and boundless contempt
while several beetles climb the window frame
and fan their wings in early evening gusts.
Although the cat observes with lazy eyes,
the gently pushing wind dips and spreads
the backyard leaves around his sleepy head.

He looks out the window to see the postman arrive, quietly stalked by next door's cat. It is Valentine's Day and he hasn't received a single valentine although his pseudo-girlfriend has received at least five. Since he does not believe, as Jack Kerouac would have it, that mother is the necessity of invention, he decides to throw himself into work. The sight of the cat and the sensual breeze reminds him, however, of his pseudo-love. He puts down his pen and has a cold shower (it is summer after all) getting ready for a barbecue that starts at six in the next suburb.

Absolutely brilliant people cluster
in loquacious nodes arbitrating
contradictions, purpled knowledge, weeds
among the loads of flowers at their feet.
Mouths on sticks and gaudy heads on stalks
sway in the tide of talk, the all too easy
colours like automatic gestures, greetings
stark against the grey yard.
It happens that the air is clear and warm,
and where the grass grows between the cracks
eyes wander, distracted, at a loss
for something smart to say. Evening comes
and conversation shrivels like a rare
Tahitian flower overpowered by the night.

He arrives at the party (to which he has been invited for a change) and meets a pride of bright young academics. He finds himself overwhelmed by words, but not at a complete loss. For instance, what is "the poetics of proprioception"? How is it done? Despite the entertaining badinage and witticisms, he observes that generally the problem with humans is that they think that because they speak in ways they understand this also means they understand themselves, their actions and what they strive to communicate, all at the same time. He manages to scoff a few sausages and some red wine before the party evaporates.

Such are the wonders of nature: almost transcendent
blue sky and a pair of crooning reptiles,
distant cousins of stone emitting alien
lullabies on a rocky altar hard
by the edge of a blind land — o desire,
flowing out of itself yet perfectly formed
each and every time, mistaken for
the song of love or fear of the sea or pity
for a becalmed ship mooning the horizon.
On other days hordes of gulls wheedle
and shriek and cold waves strike the shore.
This is the limit, where foam flies and rocks
endure the sea and various creatures slide
in and out as smoothly as machines.

The next day is decidedly ordinary. He wants to enrich his measly existence with culture-vulturing at the art gallery (he has called his pseudo-girlfriend but she is most emphatically not in.) There are some surreal works on show, Magritte's being his favourite. Before one particular painting he is transfixed — the combination of beauty, the inexplicable and the incongruously familiar almost moves him to tears. He has arranged to meet his Irish friend later at their local. From the bus the city looks as though it is populated by mad Futurists. It probably is. '

Shakespeare' is a metaphor of
our inadequacy, framing our actions
so that we cannot conceive of beating
his collective genius. If not
'Shakespeare', then what else ? Where's the tragedy
of experimental, mental, stupid
poetry, doomed because it comes
too late ? Who is asking the questions here ?
Swallow a cockroach and gag reading Henry
IV Part I and revel as with every
whiff of truth. Consort with paranoia
and what you get is pain, an overreaching
drive to cancel little setbacks, fuck
the strange ambitions that make life suck.

"And how is the journey through the vale of tears?" enquires his Irish friend. He replies noncommittally. When his friend asks after his pseudo-girlfriend he tells him that he hasn't seen her for a while. "I've never met a sentimental woman yet," he says as an oblique conversation stopper, staring at his other little friend, his beer. In the slightly embarrassed silence that ensues, their only recourse is to a general discussion of literature, their usual topic of last resort. As is to be expected, the conversation doesn't last very long and they soon part company. He picks up a few more little friends on the way home to keep him company.

Life is on the chair and on TV
they're just people, they make up and out and
break down in this cup and saucer world
and still they're at it, night after night,
flowing out from ourselves and coiling through
them like a snail's shell, growing
out as if no-one was involved at all.
Life is on the bed, caught unawares,
wasting hours that would otherwise
be wasted quite away. But sleep is never
owned, it hops from head to head, not stopping
for tiredness but unsettling the night,
lingering in the laundry of the soul
or revelling in dreams of pure excess.

He gets home late and again explores the mindless morass of late night television. It doesn't seem to matter how bad it gets as long as the commercials don't get too intrusive. Since greatness loiters in the margins of mediocrity (much as mediocrity continually pops out in surprise from behind greatness) it is as much an education as if he were watching some 'classic' of art-house cinema. In reality, neither is as enjoyable as his own private movies, his dreams, a claim he could substantiate if only one day he could actually remember one.

Music survives in air for a time then fades
and then comes back after playing possum a while.
When it has gone for good, harmonies
that merged and then divided, different voices
bickering then wheeled away, the silence
begs for that disturbance once again,
the scribble in the margins or the starling
that hops along the gutter. Before the sound
cranks up again crescent husks of leaves
scuttle in gusts across the patio
and then the slow lamenting tune begins
and will not stop and soon will not regret
the brutal rhythms walloping the walls
when unforgiving madness makes its call.

The next day happiness arrives out of nowhere and settles upon him like a snappy new suit. As he is not one to ask good fortune for its ID card he puts on some of his favourite music, although this does pose something of a dilemma – the 60s music he and his first love listened to playing happy families is out, as is the 80s music his pseudo-girlfriend prefers, leaving only a combination of 70s and 90s music, making him feel like a grooving retro-hipster. He turns up the volume on one of his favourites but when the neighbours complain he turns it down and starts rearranging his bookshelves instead.

Mirrors make the house.
Images congeal into rooms and aspects
of mortality hide behind a gaze.
Corridors appear in a frenzy of reflection
and quickly, quickly! –
the world completes itself in silver-skied
riddles and looking-glass facts.
Odours abound, of cooking
and loving and vegetable decay.
The gentleness of returned smiles
masks a deeper tenderness,
the unfinished violence of being.
And thoughts, too, are shadowed shapes
cast on the still lake of oblivion.

He has to go up the road to buy some milk, and as he comes out of the supermarket, he runs into his pseudo-girlfriend, arm in arm with another man. She looks as if she's seen a ghost, while he manages a polite "hello" before he passes by. How could he not have expected 'special friends' to end up any other way? His 'negative optimism' is in full flight — unsurprised and saddened he walks home lopping the heads of innocent flowers that have the misfortune to be on his way. He thinks of a mirror, perhaps even one in his room, reflecting when no one is there, and is moved by the simple impossibility. Obviously. if his father is anywhere to be found, it is in just such a room.

The rules decree "thou shalt be happy"
days full of tragic complexity
overwhelmed by laughter.
Too many paths that could be gone down
resolve into one path marked only by years
piled like stones by the side of the road.
Beyond ordinary meanings
other sentences unfurl themselves
like eternal flowers
dandled by the heavy breeze
breathing life into the speechless past
flatly denied by the teeming present
and passing, with forgiveness, to the future.

Aside from the fact that from time to time life seems to be a very long snuff movie, he emerges from a daydream to look at the page before him. This is what it's all about, he decides, the white page, the endless choice. On the way home he found a lobster (twenty dollar note) on the ground – O lucky day! – with which he was able to buy himself a lotto entry, a lottery ticket, some marinated olives and artichoke hearts for a salad. "When will my luck run out? " he asks himself as he eats his lunch over the sports section of the newspaper.

About the Author

David Musgrave is a poet, novelist, critic and publisher. His poetry has received numerous awards, the most recent being the Judith Wright Calanthe Award for *Anatomy of Voice* in 2016. He lives in Newcastle, NSW with his family and teaches at the University of Newcastle.

Acknowledgements

On Reflection, written in the mid-1990s, was first published by Interactive Press in 2005.

www.ingramcontent.com/pod-product-compliance
Lightning Source LLC
Chambersburg PA
CBHW030853090426
42737CB00009B/1212